English Code 4

Grammar Book

Contents

Welcome back!

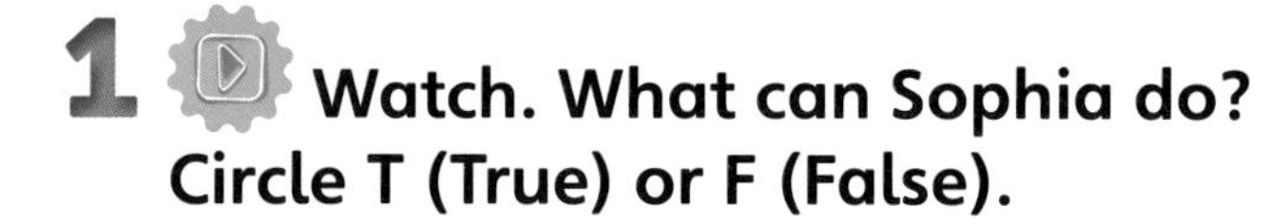

1 Watch. What can Sophia do? Circle T (True) or F (False).

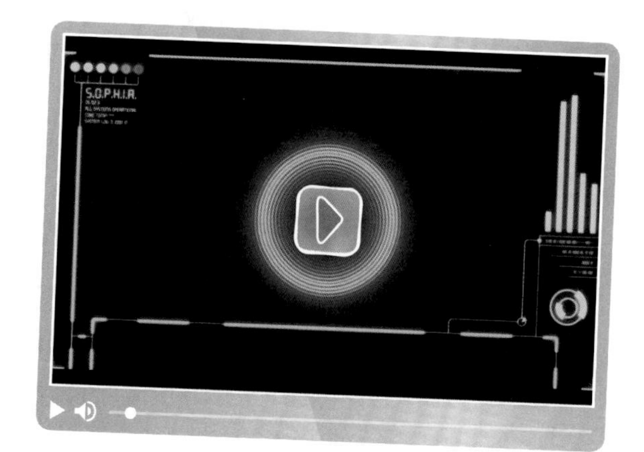

Sophia can …

1 show pictures. T / F
2 paint pictures. T / F
3 make videos. T / F
4 play music. T / F
5 change her voice. T / F

2 Who likes what? Choose and write 1 (Player 1), 2 (Player 2), or 3 (Player 3). Then watch to check. Say.

1	acting	☐	2	baking	☐
3	drawing	☐	4	going out with friends	☐
5	ice skating	☐	6	music	☐
7	painting	☐	8	reading	☐
9	running	☐	10	swimming	☐

Player 1 likes …

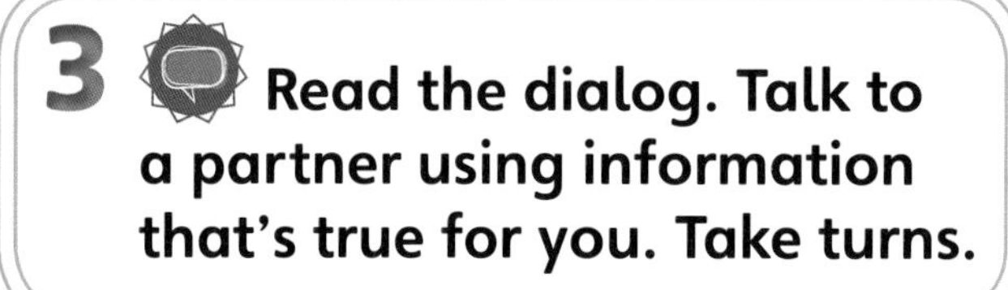

3 Read the dialog. Talk to a partner using information that's true for you. Take turns.

CODE CRACKER

Hello. I'm NAME.

Hi, NAME. What do you like doing?

I like ACTION 1 and ACTION 2.

Why do you like ACTION 1 and ACTION 2?

I like ACTION 1 because REASON 1 and I like ACTION 2 because REASON 2.

I like ACTION 1, too, but I don't like ACTION 2 because REASON 3. I like ACTION 3.

Language lab

WHEN …?

I will learn to ask and answer about dates.

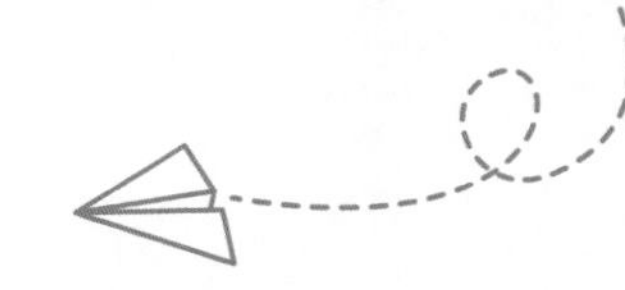

1 Read the dialog. What are Dad and Katie talking about? Check ☑.

1 Dad's birthday party ☐
2 Katie's sister's birthday party ☐
3 Katie's and Ellie's birthday party ☐

Dad: Are you OK, Katie? You look sad.
Katie: It's my birthday …
Dad: What about it? It's on May fifth. That's next week.
Katie: Yes. It's on a Thursday, so I can't have my party then. We have school.
Dad: When do you want to have your birthday party, then?
Katie: I want to have it on Saturday, on the seventh. But it's Ellie's birthday on May second. She wants to have a party on Saturday, too. She's my best friend!
Dad: Well, why don't you have a party together?
Katie: How?
Dad: You can have it on Saturday, on the seventh, in our garden.
Katie: Great idea, Dad! Thanks! Can I call Ellie now and ask her?
Dad: Sure!

When's your birthday?
It's on **January twentieth** / January 20th.
When's your party?
It's on **December third** / December 3rd.

2 Read again. Circle the correct dates.

1 When is Katie's birthday?
It's on May second / fifth / seventh .
2 When does Katie want to have a party?
She wants to have a party on May second / fifth / seventh .
3 When is Ellie's birthday?
It's on May second / fifth / seventh .
4 When does Ellie want to have a party?
She wants to have a party on May second / fifth / seventh .
5 When are Katie and Ellie going to have a party?
They are going to have a party on May second / fifth / seventh .

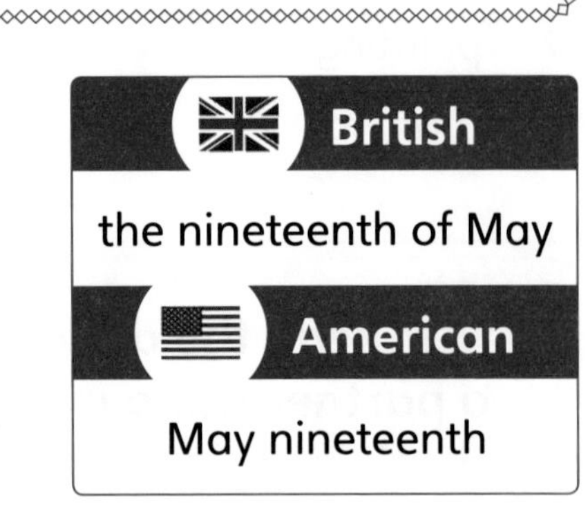

3 Read the dialog again. Underline a question with when.

4 Look and complete the answers.

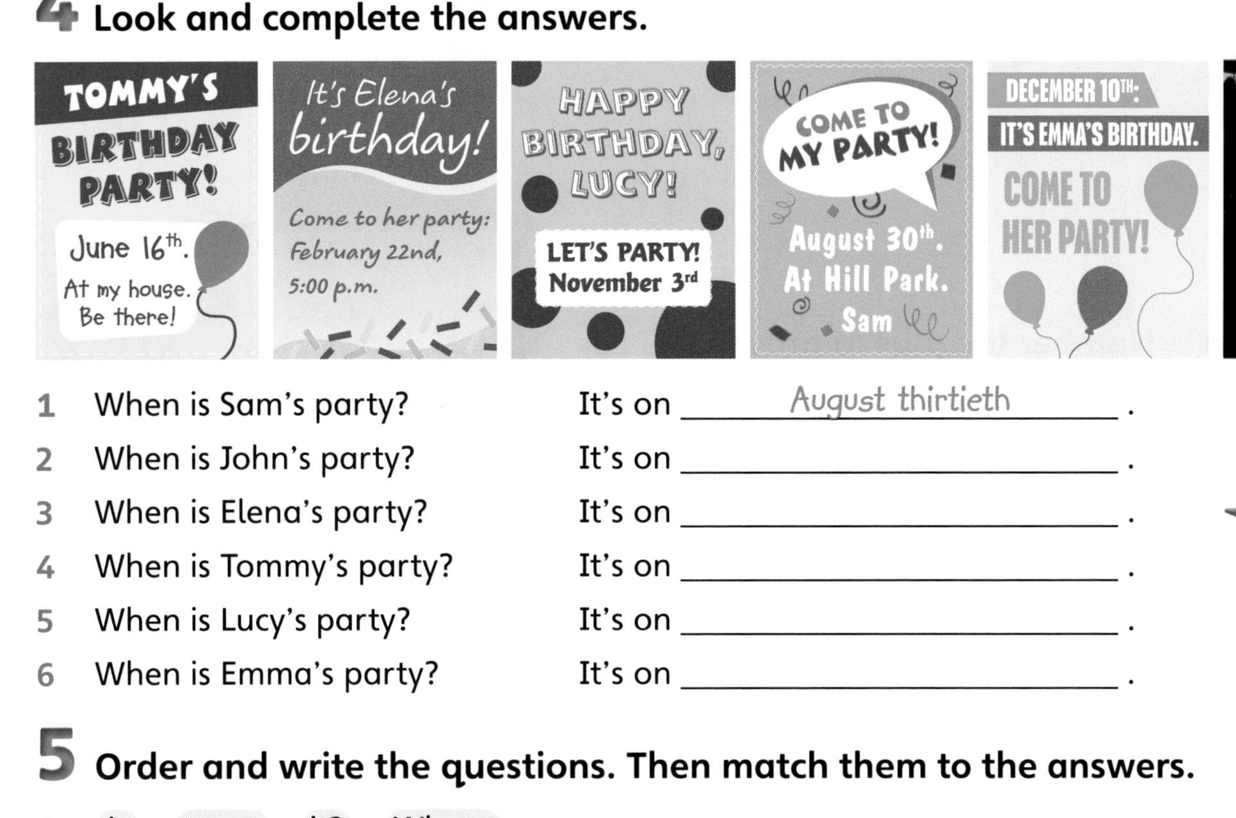

1 When is Sam's party? It's on August thirtieth.
2 When is John's party? It's on ______________.
3 When is Elena's party? It's on ______________.
4 When is Tommy's party? It's on ______________.
5 When is Lucy's party? It's on ______________.
6 When is Emma's party? It's on ______________.

5 Order and write the questions. Then match them to the answers.

1 is party it? Whose
______________ ☐

2 is When birthday? his
______________ ☐

3 his When party? is
______________ ☐

4 the is party? Where
______________ ☐

a The birthday's on July ninth.
b It's at Daniel's house.
c Daniel's
d The party's on July eleventh.

6 Make a birthday invitation for a friend or someone in your family. Show it to a partner. Ask and answer questions.

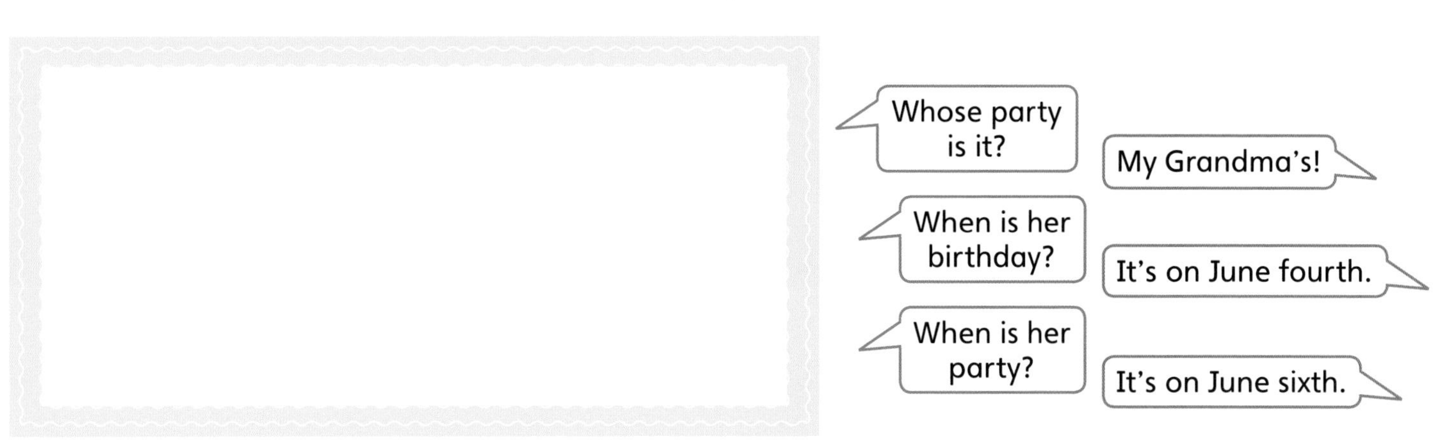

1 Into the wild

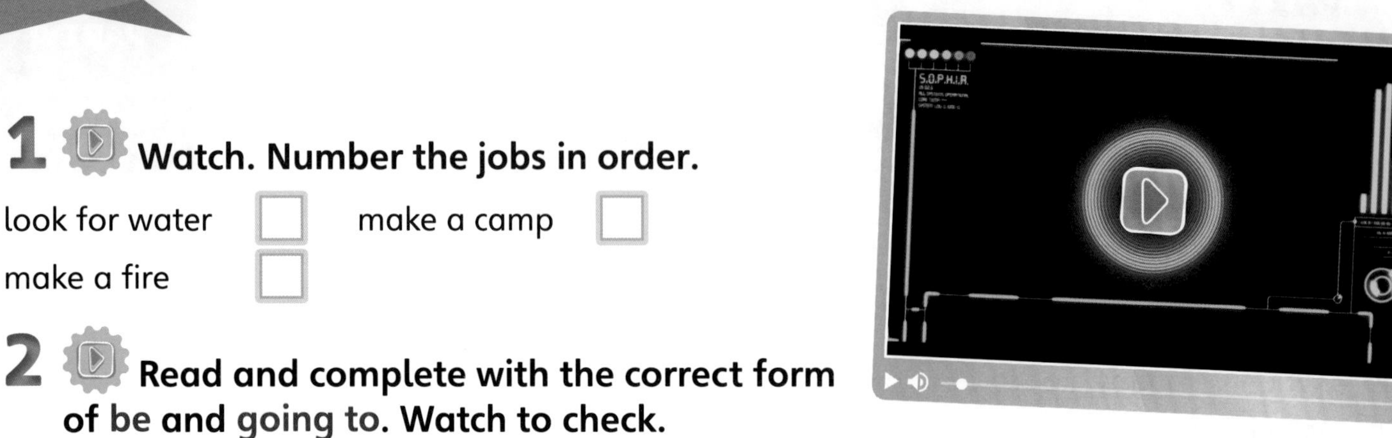

1 Watch. Number the jobs in order.

look for water ☐ make a camp ☐

make a fire ☐

2 Read and complete with the correct form of be and going to. Watch to check.

1 They ________________ do a challenge.
2 Player 1 ________________ make a fire.
3 She ________________ make a roof.
4 Player 2 ________________ look for water.
5 He ________________ look for shelter.
6 Player 3 ________________ make a bed.
7 She ________________ make a camp.

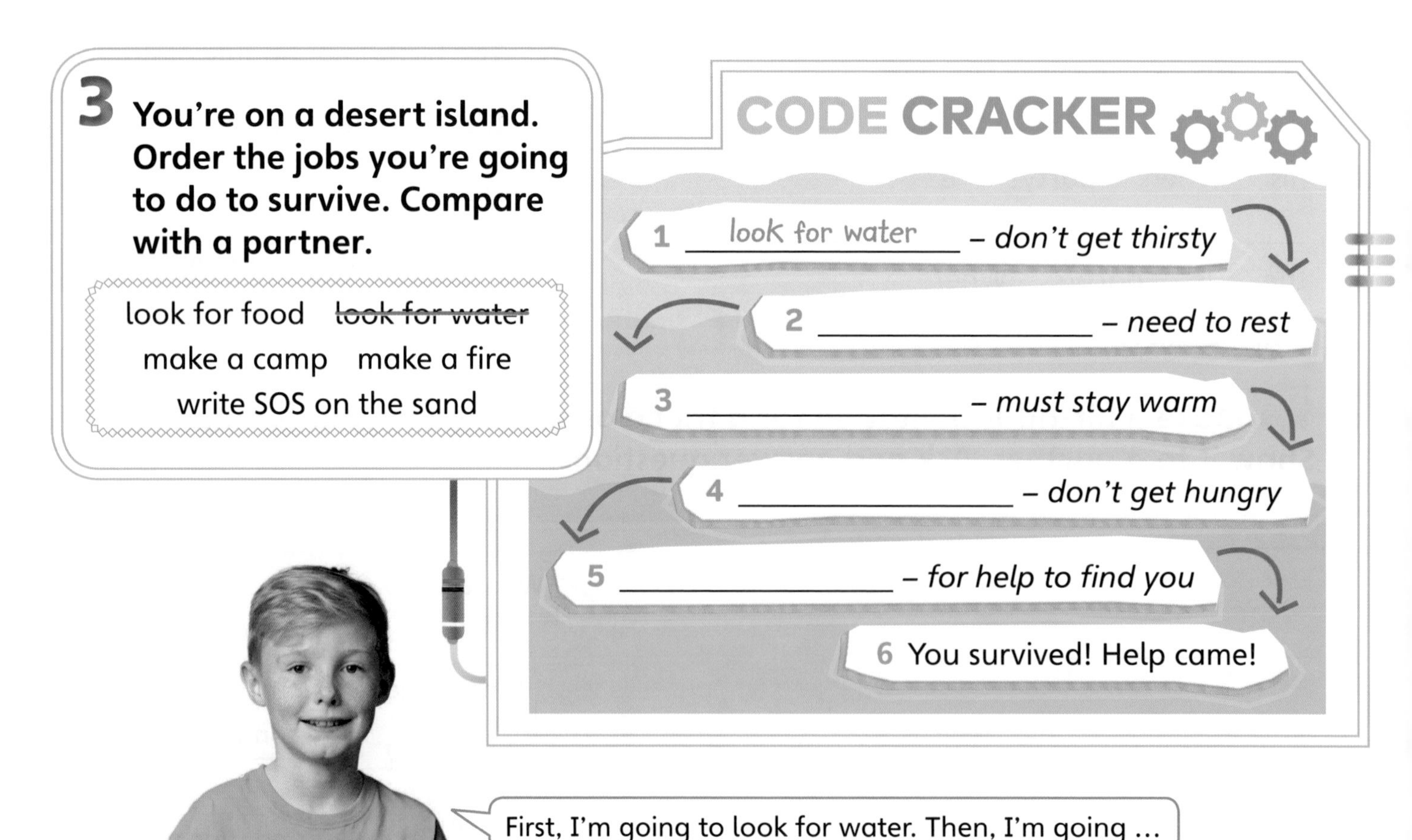

3 You're on a desert island. Order the jobs you're going to do to survive. Compare with a partner.

look for food ~~look for water~~
make a camp make a fire
write SOS on the sand

CODE CRACKER

1 look for water – *don't get thirsty*
2 ________________ – *need to rest*
3 ________________ – *must stay warm*
4 ________________ – *don't get hungry*
5 ________________ – *for help to find you*
6 You survived! Help came!

First, I'm going to look for water. Then, I'm going …

Language lab 1

GOING TO ...

I will learn to talk about future plans using ***going to.***

1 Read the messages. What are Sam and David going to do this weekend? Check ☑ the correct photos.

a 

b 

c 

d 

Dear Sam,

It's great that you're going to visit on Saturday. What time are you going to get here? We can meet you at the bus station.

I'm sorry, but we can't go to the beach because my parents are busy. They're going to work in the garden in the morning. My dad's going to cut some branches and my mom's going to pick up the leaves. Maybe we can help them? For lunch, we're going to have a picnic in the forest near our house. Don't forget to bring your boots!

Bye,

David

Hi, David!

That sounds great! I love walking in the forest and looking at insects. I'm going to bring my boots and my compass, too. OK? And yes, let's help your mom and dad.

I'm not going to take the bus. My mom's going to drive me to your house. We're going to be there at about ten o'clock and she's going to pick me up at eight o'clock in the evening.

See you on Saturday!

Sam

2 Who are the sentences about? Write D (*David*), S (*Sam*), or B (*both*).

1 He's going to arrive at ten o'clock. ____
2 He isn't going to go to the beach. ____
3 His parents are going to work in the garden. ____
4 He's going to have a picnic in the forest. ____

I'**m going to** have a picnic.

We / You'**re going to** take the train.

He'**s not going to** study.

They **aren't going to** watch a movie.

Are you **going to** see your uncle?
Yes, we **are**. / No, we **aren't**.

What **are** you **going to** do on Sunday?

3 Read the messages again. Underline questions and sentences with going to.

4 Circle the correct answer.

1 It's cold today, so I am going / am not going to go for a walk.
2 We're going to / go to use a compass in the forest. Great!
3 How are you / you are going to cross the stream?
4 Tim needs new gloves. He is to / is going to go shopping tomorrow.
5 **A:** Are they / Do they going to make a treehouse in their garden?
B: Yes, they are going / are .

5 Read the text. Complete it with the words in the box.

Are be going going to isn't 're 're going to

I'm Lisa and I'm 1 ___________ to act with the School Drama Club this year. I'm so happy! Our teacher is Mr. Ellis. He chose a play about a family's vacation that doesn't go well. They travel by boat and get to a desert island. It's called *Waiting for help*. We 2 ___________ going to perform it at the end of the school year. It's a funny play. I'm going 3 ___________ be the mother and my friend Mike is going to 4 ___________ the son. We're 5 ___________ have real costumes! The boat 6 ___________ going to be real, but we 7 ___________ to use ropes and a compass. It's going to be great! 8 ___________ you going to come and see the play?

6 Complete the questions.

1 ___________ you ___________ go to the park after school?
2 ___________ your dad/mom ___________ make pizza for dinner?
3 ___________ your dad/mom ___________ drive you to school tomorrow?
4 ___________ your friends ___________ play basketball on Friday?
5 ___________ you ___________ see a friend this weekend?

7 Ask a partner the questions in 6. Write the answers.

1 ____.
2 ____.
3 ____.
4 ____.
5 ____.

Language lab 2

TIME PHRASES

I will ask and answer about future plans.

1 Read. Circle the time words and phrases.

I'm going to start high school in September! I'm so happy! I have new clothes and I'm going to buy a new bag on Saturday. I'm going to go to the mall with my friend, Sally, at eleven o'clock. She's going to arrive tomorrow and she's going to stay at my house for three days.

Time phrases

at + time

on + day

in + month

for + amount of time

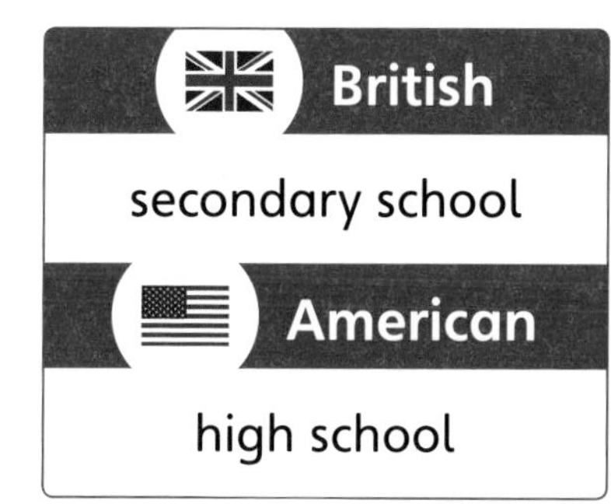

British	American
secondary school	high school

2 Complete the sentences with the words in the box.

at for in on tomorrow

1 Emma's going to sleep in a tent __________ seven days.

2 It's going to rain __________ Friday. We can't go swimming.

3 Are your parents going to cut the grass __________ ? Let's help them!

4 **A:** What time is Fred going to arrive?

B: __________ four o'clock.

5 We're going to go camping __________ August. We need a new compass!

3 Write the questions in order. Then ask and answer with a partner using time phrases.

What time ...?

At nine o'clock.

Me too!

1 you What time tonight? to go to bed are going

____

2 going grandparents? are to see you your When

____

3 to going you are be this summer? How long at the science camp

____

4 are When finish school going you this year? to

____

2 Into the past

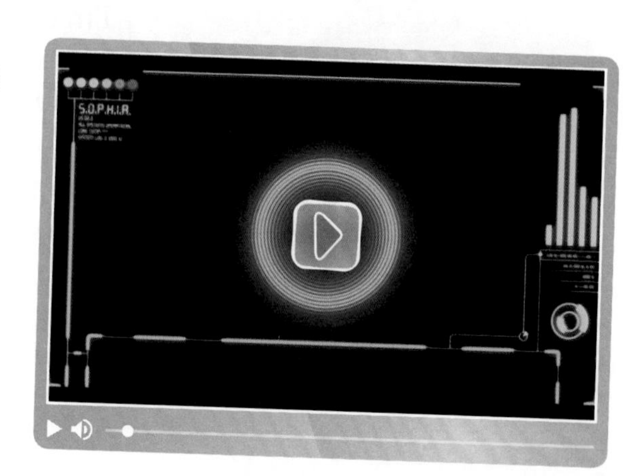

1 Watch. Check ☑ the topics the players talk about with Sophia.

jewelry	☐	sports	☐
language	☐	cities	☐
food	☐	drinks	☐

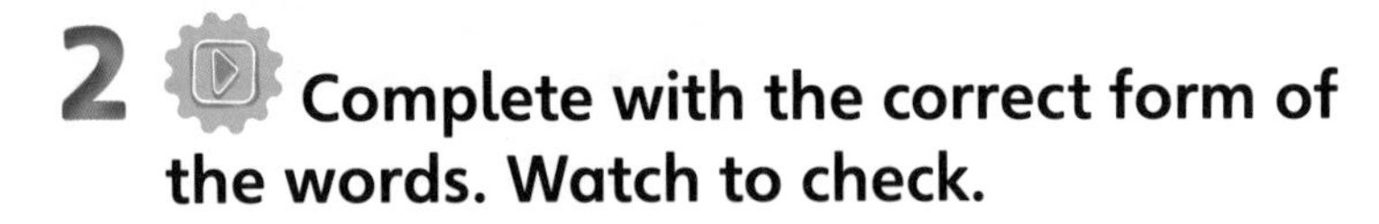

2 Complete with the correct form of the words. Watch to check.

drink eat speak

1 The Mayans __________ chili peppers, beans, and maize.
2 People in Mexico __________ Spanish.
3 The Mayans __________ spicy hot chocolate.

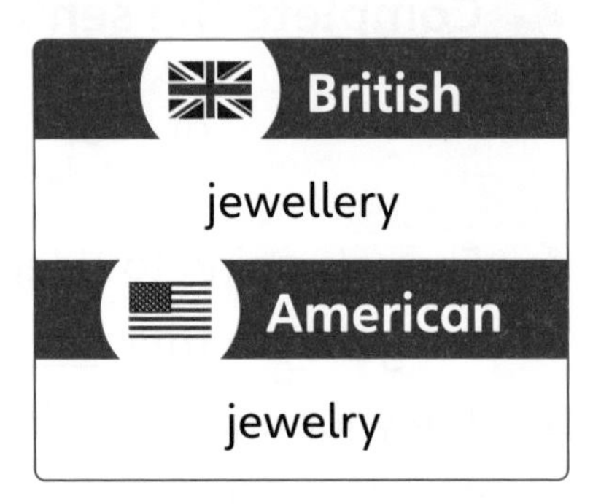

British
jewellery
American
jewelry

3 Read the sentences about the ancient Mayans and about Mexicans now. Check ☑ the correct ones.

CODE CRACKER

1 They all spoke Mayan AND they all spoke Spanish. ☐
2 They built cities with pyramids BUT they didn't build museums. ☐
3 Some people work in the fields AND some people work in cities. ☐
4 They wore tunics AND they wore T-shirts. ☐
5 They ate maize and beans AND they drank hot chocolate. ☐
6 They play soccer BUT they don't play basketball. ☐

Language lab 1

PAST AND PRESENT

I will learn to compare the past and the present.

1 Read the text. Who won the Artist of the Year award?

Matías Acosta ☐ Carla Garcia ☐ Jack Sun ☐

Matías Acosta was a soccer player. He played for some of the best clubs around the world. He played as a forward and he was a team captain for Brazil. He won the Player of the Year award in 2015. He's a coach now.

Carla Garcia is a high school student, but she is also a famous writer. She won an award for Best Young Writer in 2018 for her book *Aztec Pyramid*. Her books are for young people between 12 and 15 years old. She also travels a lot and helps poor people around the world.

Jack Sun is a Canadian singer. He was born in Toronto. His first album came out in 2017 and he won the Artist of the Year award in 2018. Young people like him a lot, but he has a lot of older fans as well. He travels a lot and helps many international organizations. They build schools and hospitals in poor countries.

2 Read again. Write T (True) or F (False).

1 Matías played for a Brazilian soccer team. ___
2 Carla Garcia writes books for very young children. ___
3 Jack Sun sang in schools and hospitals. ___

3 Read again. Underline sentences that talk about the past.

Present	Past
He **plays** soccer every Monday.	He **played** soccer last Monday.
She **doesn't write** songs.	She **didn't write** a book last year.
Do they **listen** to Jack Sun? Yes, they **do**. / No, they **don't**.	**Did** they **listen** to Jack Sun last week? Yes, they **did**. / No, they **didn't**.

4 Circle the correct answer.

1 Kelly study / studies Spanish at school.
2 Sarah and Jane often watch / watches Mexican movies.
3 The ancient Aztecs wear / wore gold jewelry.
4 Helen and I don't often eat / ate maize.

5 Put the words in order. You need to change the form of some words.

1 drink You cocoa never

______________________________ .

2 wear I yesterday sandals

______________________________ .

3 summer Mexico go He every to

______________________________ .

4 movie last act a year in She

______________________________ .

6 Read and complete with the correct form of the words in the box.

drink go (2) not buy not wake up swim

Every summer

1 Amanda ____________________ to the beach.
2 She ____________________ in the ocean.
3 She ____________________ early.

Last summer

1 Amanda ____________________ to Mexico City.
2 She ____________________ fresh juice for breakfast.
3 She ____________________ jewelry because it cost a lot of money.

7 Write about your favorite singer, writer, or sports star. Write about why he or she is famous and what he or she did in the past. Then share the information in groups.

My favorite ________________ is ____________________________ .

He/She ____

____

In the past, he/she ____

____

____

Language lab 2

COULD AND AGO

I will ask and answer using could and ago.

1 Read. What's Grandma's problem? Check ☑.

1 She doesn't have an oven. ☐
2 She wants to take a picture. ☐
3 She can't send a message. ☐

Grandma: Hi, Betty, what's that noise? Is that your brother?
Betty: Yes, it's Mike. He's cooking. He's putting a cake in the oven.
Grandma: Good. Sixty years ago, when I was little, I couldn't make cakes. We didn't have an oven.
Betty: You have one now, Grandma.
Grandma: I know and I love it! I made your favorite cookies yesterday.
Betty: Yummy! Sorry we couldn't visit you yesterday. We were at school.
Grandma: OK. Can you come now? I have a problem with my phone. I took a picture of the cookies yesterday and I couldn't send it to you.
Betty: Grandma, did you press "send"?
Grandma: Yes, I did! Sixty years ago, we didn't have smartphones, but we could send letters. That was easier.
Betty: Yes, you always say that. I'll come over after lunch. OK?
Grandma: Thank you, Betty. Bye!

2 Read and circle.

1 Betty's grandma could / couldn't make cakes sixty years ago.
2 Betty's grandma could / couldn't take a picture.
3 People could / couldn't send letters sixty years ago.

Sixty years **ago**, people **could write** letters, but they couldn't send emails.

3 What could or couldn't people do in the 1960s? Look at the photos and write sentences. Then compare with a partner.

1 Many years ago, in 1960s, people ______________________________ .
2 They ______________________________ .
3 ______________________________ .

1 travel by airplane

2 make a video call

3 swim in a swimming pool

3 Up into space

1 Watch. Which questions does the Avatar answer? Check ☑.

1 What will people eat in space? ☐
2 Where will we live in space? ☐
3 Who will people meet in space? ☐
4 How will we sleep in space? ☐

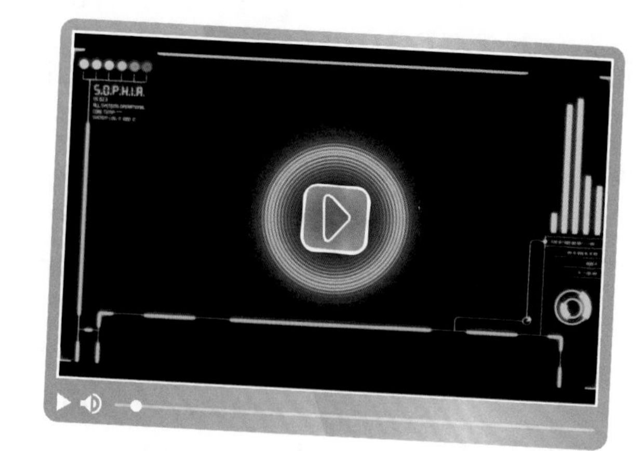

2 Read and circle. Watch to check.

1 How will / are / won't we do that, Avatar?
2 You are / will / won't wear a special dream helmet like this.
3 But in space, you will / won't / are cook food.
4 In space, you will eat / eat / won't eat the same food you eat on Earth, but it won't / is / will be made differently.

3 Read and follow the instructions.

CODE CRACKER

STEP 1: Read and order to make a dialog.

a	A:	When do you think people will live in space?	1
b	A:	Will it cost a lot to travel on these buses?	
c	A:	Where will people live in space?	
d	A:	How do you think they'll get to the space colonies?	
e	B:	They'll travel there by space buses.	
f	B:	I think they'll live in space in 2200.	
g	B:	They will live in space colonies.	
h	B:	No, it won't. It will cost $100.	

STEP 2: Practice the dialog in pairs. Use your own ideas to complete the answers.

Language lab 1

WILL AND *WON'T*

I will learn to talk about the future using ***will***.

1 Read the text. What's Olympus Mons? Check ☑.

a spaceship ☐ a planet ☐ a volcano ☐

Will people like you and me ever travel to space? Scientists believe that spaceships will be ready in 40 years to take us on vacation. These spaceships will carry tourists to amazing places, such as the Moon and even other planets. But they won't fly to other galaxies because they're too far away.

Scientists also say that the first astronauts will soon land on Mars (the Red Planet). There will be small teams of only four to six astronauts in the beginning. First, they'll explore the surface of Mars, then they'll visit Olympus Mons, the tallest volcano in the solar system. One day, there will also be a special space colony on Mars!

But will space travel really be possible for everyone one day? I'm sure it will. The only problem is it will cost a lot. So, you should start saving money now!

2 Read again. Write *Yes* or *No*.

1 The spaceships will only take astronauts on vacation.

____

2 They will carry tourists to the Sun.

____

3 It will be possible to go to Mars soon.

____

4 You will need a lot of money to fly to space.

____

3 Read again. Underline will, 'll, and won't.

I'**ll** go on a vacation to space.

They'**ll** explore Mars.

She **won't** live on Mars.

We **won't** travel to the Sun.

Will you live in a space colony?
Yes, I **will**. / No, I **won't**.

Will they walk on the Moon?
Yes, they **will**. / No, they **won't**.

will not = won't

4 Put the words in order.

1 be cheap Space travel won't

____.

2 fly to they other Will planets

____?

3 learn about the We Red Planet will

____.

5 Look at the pictures and complete the sentences with the correct form of the words in parentheses.

1 Scott ______________ (fly) in a spaceship one day. He wants to be an astronaut.

2 Astronauts ______________ (not/explore) Mars this year.

3 Do you think you ______________ (travel) to other planets one day?

4 We ______________ (need) a lot of money because space travel ______________ (not/be) cheap.

5 I ______________ (not/go) on vacation to space because I don't like flying!

6 What will our world be like in 2080? Talk with a partner. Use your ideas and the ideas in the box.

cities on other planets | festivals on the Moon | flights to the Sun | flying cars | houses on Mars | robots

There will be robots in 2080. They will clean people's houses.

In 2080, we won't have flying cars.

Language lab 2

QUESTIONS WITH *WILL*

*I will ask and answer about the future using **will**.*

1 Read. Underline the question words.

Where will you go?
When will you arrive?
What will you do?
How will you get there?
Why will you go there?

Lucas: Hi, Jack. What are you doing?
Jack: I'm reading about space travel. I'll go on vacation to space one day.
Lucas: Where will you go?
Jack: I'll go to Saturn.
Lucas: How will you get there?
Jack: On a spaceship. It'll be like a bus.
Lucas: And why will you go there?
Jack: Because I think it's an interesting planet.
Lucas: OK. What will you do there?
Jack: I'll make videos of its rings and moons. Saturn has more than 60 moons!

2 Complete the questions with the correct question word.

1 **A:** __________ will you take with you?
B: I'll take my mom and dad.

2 **A:** __________ will you go on vacation?
B: We'll go to Mars.

3 **A:** __________ will you see?
B: We'll see other planets.

4 **A:** __________ will you travel there?
B: We'll go there by spaceship.

3 Read the answers and write the questions.

1 **A:** ______________________________?
B: They'll see a big moon.

2 **A:** ______________________________?
B: We'll arrive in March 2050.

3 **A:** ______________________________?
B: She'll live in a space colony.

4 **A:** ______________________________?
B: He'll eat dry fish and special bread.

4 Dragons

1 Watch. Check ☑ the action words you can hear.

burn	☐	run	☐	sleep	☐
fly	☐	shout	☐	walk	☐

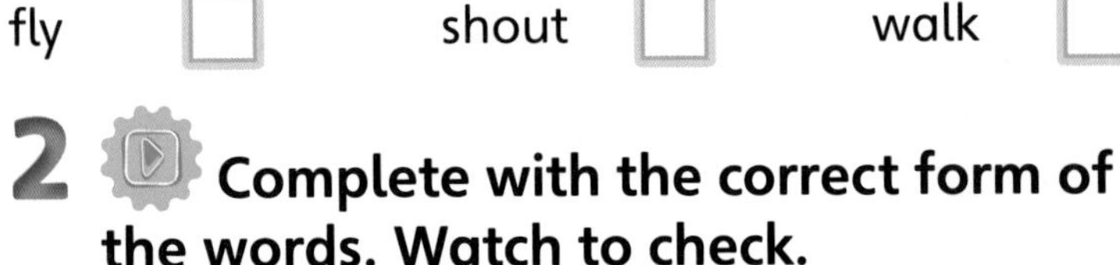

2 Complete with the correct form of the words. Watch to check.

1 The dragon was ___________ (sleep) on the grass.

2 The yellow dragon was ___________ (fly) above the castle.

3 The men were ___________ (shout) and the horses were ___________ (run) into the forest.

3 Read and complete with was/were and the correct word from 2.

CODE CRACKER

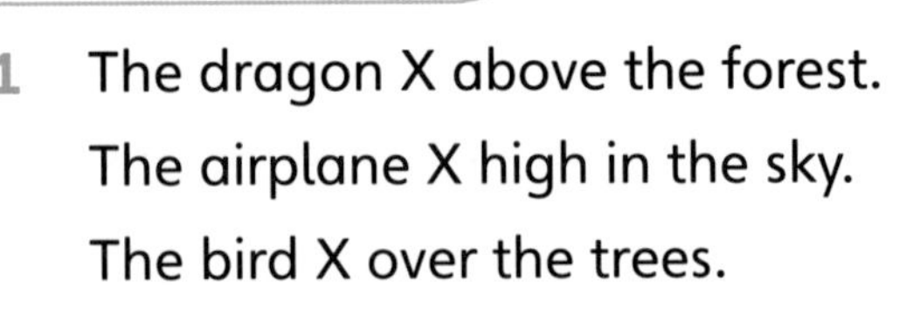

1 The dragon X above the forest.
The airplane X high in the sky.
The bird X over the trees.

X = ___________________

2 Tim and Daisy Y in a race.
The horses Y on the beach.
The men Y from the dragon.

Y = ___________________

Language lab 1

ACTIVITIES IN THE PAST

I will learn to talk about activities in the past.

1 Read. What's the message of the story? Check ☑.

1 Be kind to younger people because they need your help. ☐
2 Even strong people need help from others. ☐
3 It's easy to make friends with people who are different. ☐

One day a big, lazy dragon was sleeping under a tree. He was dreaming of lunch. A little mouse ran out of the bushes and woke the dragon. The dragon caught the mouse and smiled. "Hello. You're my lunch," he said.

"Please don't hurt me," cried the mouse. "I can help you if you let me go."

The dragon thought it was funny, so he let the mouse go.

A few days later, the king and his men were walking in the forest. They weren't looking for small animals. They wanted to catch big animals and take them to the castle. They saw the dragon and they caught him in a net.

The same mouse was walking through the forest when he heard the dragon's roar. He ran fast to help the dragon. He saw the dragon was under the net. He wasn't smiling this time. He was trying to get out, but he couldn't. "I can help," said the mouse, and he started to bite at one of the ropes of the net. Soon, the dragon was free. No kindness is ever a waste!

2 Read again. Match questions and answers.

1 What was the dragon doing at the beginning?
2 Who caught the dragon?
3 Why did the dragon let the mouse go free?
4 Was the dragon roaring when he was trapped?
5 How did the mouse help the dragon get free?

a He bit through the ropes.
b He was dreaming of food.
c Yes, he was.
d He thought the mouse was funny.
e The king and his men.

3 Read again. Underline positive action words with *-ing* in blue and negative action words with *-ing* in green.

I **was sleeping** in the forest.

They **weren't looking** for small animals.

Was he **dreaming** of food?
Yes, he **was**. / No, he **wasn't**.

What **was** the mouse **doing**?

4 Circle the correct word.

1. A dragon was flying / flying above the castle.
2. I wasn't feel / feeling very hungry.
3. Was she reading / read a book about animals yesterday evening?
4. The dragon and the mouse weren't / wasn't sleeping in the forest.
5. The children were watch / watching a movie about a dragon.

5 What's different? Read and match to make the rules.

1. He was dreaming of something nice.
2. It wasn't running.
3. They were walking in the jungle.
4. We weren't watching TV.

We use *was/wasn't* with •

We use *were/weren't* with •

• *you*, *we*, and *they*.

• *I*, *he*, *she*, and *it*.

6 Draw and write a short dragon story. Act out your stories in groups.

TITLE: ______________________________

1

____

____

2

____

____

3

____

____

4

____

____

Language lab 2

EVENTS IN THE PAST

I will ask and answer about events in the past.

1 Read. How many misadventures did Jane have? Write.

_____ misadventures

Jane's 9 years old and she has a lot of misadventures every day! On Sunday, she was playing with a ball in the hall when she kicked it and broke a window. Jane said "I'm sorry," to her mom and dad. On Monday, she was making a paper dragon and using a glue stick in her dad's office when she got glue all over his papers. He wasn't happy! On Tuesday, she was riding her bike to school when she fell. She was wearing a helmet, so she was OK. On Wednesday, she was playing soccer in the yard with her brother when she kicked his ball over the roof. They looked for it but they couldn't find it. Then on Thursday, she was studying in the library when she lost her toy dragon. Now she needs to buy a new toy dragon. It's Friday. What will happen to Jane today?

2 Read and circle T (True) or F (False).

1 Jane was studying in the library when she lost her bag. T / F
2 She was wearing a helmet when she fell off her bike. T / F
3 Jane was playing with a ball when she broke a window. T / F
4 She got paint on her dad's papers. T / F
5 Jane and her brother were playing soccer when they lost the ball. T / F

3 Complete with the correct form of the action words.

1 She ________________ (eat) lunch when she ________________ (drop) her sandwich.
2 I ________________ (run) in the yard when I ________________ (fall) over.
3 We ________________ (watch) a movie when the lights ________________ (go) out.
4 You ________________ (not play) soccer when Natalie ________________ (arrive).

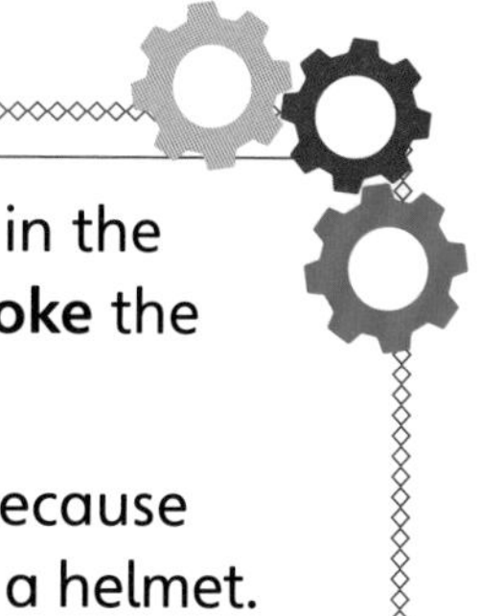

She **was playing** in the hall when she **broke** the window.

I **hurt** my head because I **wasn't wearing** a helmet.

What **were** they **doing** when you **saw** them?

5 Endangered animals

1 Watch. Which animals do they talk about? Check ☑ or cross ☒.

a

b

c

d

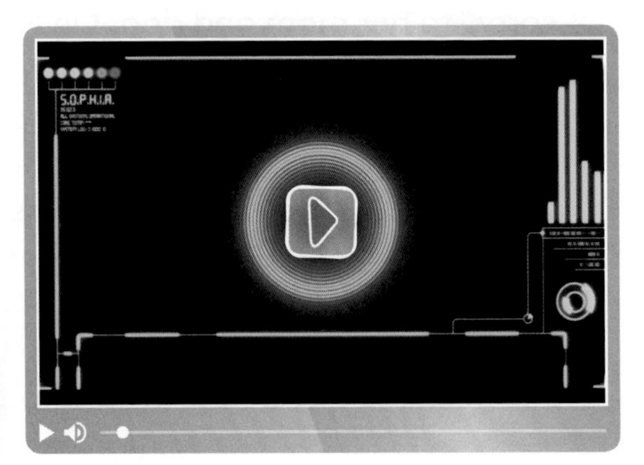

2 Read and circle. Watch to check.

1 If they destroy / will destroy the forest, the tigers lose / will lose their home.
2 If they don't clean up / won't clean up the river, the fish die / will die.
3 If we use / will use fewer chemicals, we have / will have more butterflies.

3 Continue the chain of ideas.

CODE CRACKER

→ If they don't clean up the river, the fish will die.
If the fish die, the bears will get very hungry.
If the bears get very hungry, ______________________.
If ______________________, ______________________.
If ______________________, ______________________.

Language lab 1

***IF* … SENTENCES**

I will learn to use sentences with *if*.

1 Read the dialog. Where will the family go for their vacation? Check ☑.

Water Fun ☐ Animal World ☐

Dad: We need to decide about our summer vacation. Where can we go?

Sally: Can we go to Water Fun? It's going to be great!

Mom: If we go to Water Fun, you and your brother will be in the swimming pool all day.

Billy: I want to see animals. Let's go to Animal World.

Sally: What's that?

Billy: You can walk in a jungle and see different kinds of animals. There are also some endangered animals. Mom, you'll love it!

Dad: What do you say, Connie? It sounds interesting.

Mom: Yes. If we go there, you'll learn about habitats of endangered animals and threats to wildlife.

Billy: We can hike up a mountain, too. And we can go down a river to see a real rainforest there!

Sally: Wow!

Dad: It sounds amazing!

Mom: OK, so we all agree.

2 Read and complete with one or two words.

1 The family are talking about their ______________________ vacation.
2 Sally would like to go to a place with a ______________________ .
3 Billy wants to go to a place with ______________________ .
4 In Animal World, they'll learn about ______________________ animals.
5 If they go to Animal World, they will see a real ______________________ .

3 Read again. Underline the sentences with if.

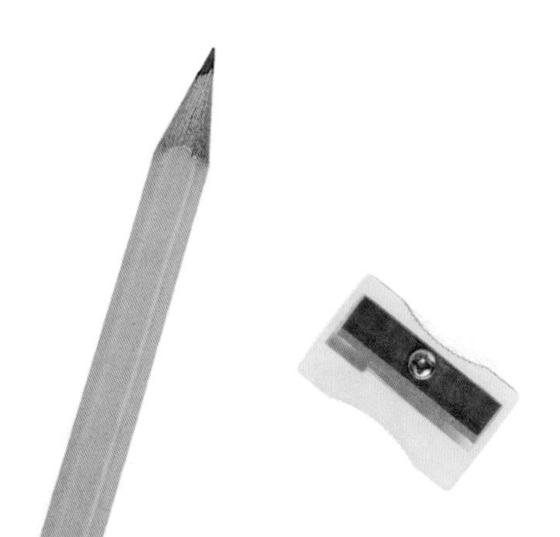

If we **visit** the rainforest, we'**ll see** beautiful butterflies.

If we **pollute** the river, otters **won't have** food.

Will they **use** chemicals if we **tell** them there are endangered animals?

4 Match to make sentences.

1 If I buy this book about animals,
2 If they plant more trees in our town,
3 She won't see any animals
4 If they build a new playground,
5 I will travel to the Amazon this summer
6 Dad won't take us to the mountain

a there won't be so much pollution.
b if I pass my exams.
c if we don't promise to be good.
d if she isn't quiet.
e I'll learn more about them.
f we will have a place to play after school.

5 Complete with the correct form of the words in parentheses.

1 If you ________________ (visit) the Ottery Wildlife Center, you'll see real otters!
2 There ________________ (not/be) any tigers left if we don't protect them.
3 Will the fish die if we ________________ (not/pollute) the rivers anymore?
4 If you want to see a turtle on the beach tomorrow, you ________________ (need to) wake up early.
5 If I ________________ (go) to the forest, where will I see butterflies?
6 Our planet ________________ (be) cleaner if we recycle trash.

6 Complete about your partner. Ask your partner if you guessed correctly.

1 You'll feel good/bad if ________________________________ .
2 If you see a wolf one day, ________________________________ .
3 If you go to the mountains, ________________________________ .
4 You'll be happy if ________________________________ .
5 If you get a good grade on the exam, ________________________________ .

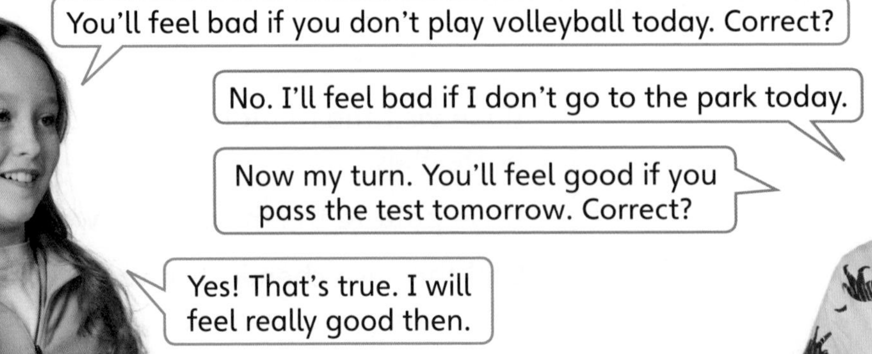

Language lab 2

MORE OR *FEWER*?

1 Read. What threats are there to humpback whales? Check ☑.

buses ☐ dolphins ☐ fishing boats ☐ warmer seas ☐

Humpback whales are beautiful, big animals. They can be as big as a school bus! They don't stay in the same place all year, but they swim all over the world to find warm waters. There are fewer humpback whales today than in 1940, when there were many. Some of the threats to humpback whales are that there are more fishing boats, and whales get caught in the nets. There are also fewer dolphins now than before the 1980s, when the dolphin population was big. It's because of these boats, too. The humpback whales eat small fish and plankton. There are fewer fish and plankton than there were some years ago because the sea temperature is changing.

Humpback whale

2 Read again and circle more or fewer.

1 There were more / fewer humpback whales in 1940 than today.

2 There are more / fewer dolphins now than before the 1980s.

3 There are more / fewer fishing boats and nets today than 40 years ago.

4 Humpback whales need to eat more / fewer small fish and plankton than they eat now.

3 Complete the dialog with more or fewer.

Are there **fewer** whales now **than** fifty years ago?

There are **more** threats to whales today **than** fifty years ago.

Tom: Look! There are so many butterflies.

Lisa: Yes, there are 1 __________ butterflies in spring than in winter. Are there a lot of butterflies where you live?

Tom: No, because people are using 2 __________ chemicals in the fields.

Lisa: Chemicals are bad for butterflies.

Tom: I know … There are even 3 __________ snails and snakes than butterflies. I never see any.

Lisa: What animals are there where you live?

Tom: There are otters and eagles. There are 4 __________ otters now than before because people are taking care of them.

Lisa: And what about eagles?

Tom: There are 5 __________ eagles than before because they don't have food.

Lisa: That's bad!

6 Join in!

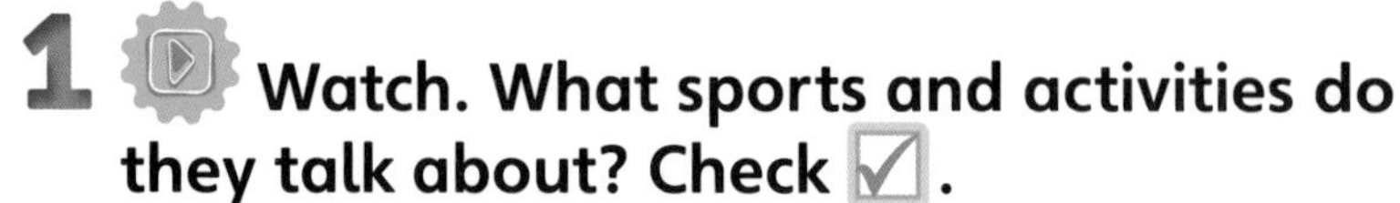

1 Watch. What sports and activities do they talk about? Check ☑.

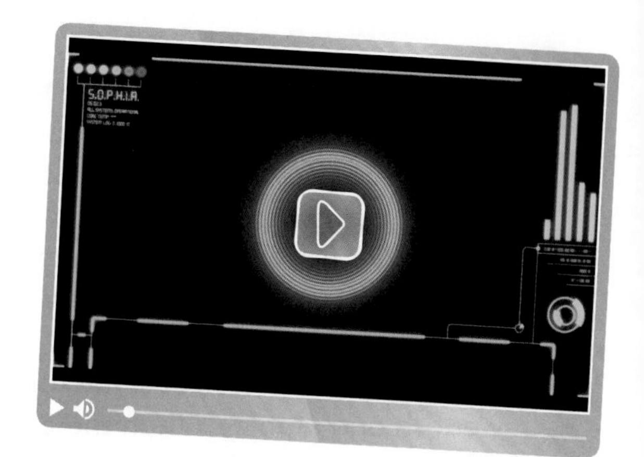

dancing	☐	soccer	☐
ice skating	☐	singing in a choir	☐
going on a boat trip	☐	swimming	☐

2 Read and circle should or shouldn't. Watch to check.

1 You should / shouldn't kick the ball into the goal to score.
2 You should / shouldn't touch the ball with your hand.
3 You should / shouldn't kick the ball to your teammates.
4 You should / shouldn't listen to the conductor.
5 You should / shouldn't talk when you're not singing.
6 You should / shouldn't stand up straight when you sing.

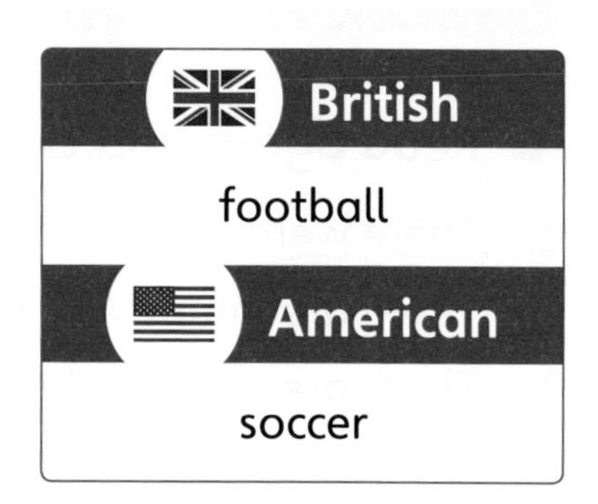

3 Read and rewrite the sentences if the information is wrong. Check ☑ the correct ones.

CODE CRACKER

1 In basketball, you should kick the ball. ☐

____

2 In a choir, you shouldn't dance faster than the other children. ☐

____

3 In soccer, you shouldn't touch the ball with your hands. ☐

____

4 In a chess club, you shouldn't be nice to other players. ☐

____

Language lab 1

SHOULD ALWAYS OR NEVER

I will learn to talk about rules using ***should.***

1 Read the messages. Match them to the replies.

1. I'm Sam. We moved to a new neighborhood and I want to join your chess club. What rules are there? ☐

2. My name's Lucy and I want to join the drama club. I sometimes perform for my family at home. What do I need to know about the club? ☐

3. This is Claire. I often play table tennis at home. Can I join the school table tennis team? What should I do? ☐

a. You shouldn't buy a racket. Our club has rackets for all team members. You should always wear sneakers and sports clothes. You should play with everyone in the club.

b. You should always come to play chess on Mondays and Wednesdays. You shouldn't leave the pieces on the table when you finish playing and you should never shout.

c. You should be at the club at twelve o'clock on Saturdays. You should always listen to the director and you should never be afraid to ask questions. You should learn your part.

2 Read again. Circle T (True) or F (False).

1. Sam shouldn't go to the club on Tuesdays. T / F
2. He should speak loudly. T / F
3. Claire should use a racket from the club. T / F
4. She should wear jeans. T / F
5. Lucy should go to the club after twelve o'clock. T / F

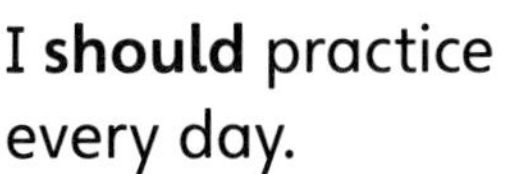

I **should** practice every day.

We **shouldn't** meet in the evening.

You **should always** be kind to teammates.

She **should never** be late for a meeting.

3 Read again. Underline the sentences with **should/shouldn't** and **always/never.**

Remember!

always ✓✓✓✓✓

often ✓✓✓

sometimes ✓✓

never ✗

She always practices with her team.

4 Put the words in order.

1 often the Nick trash empties

______________________________.

2 practice teammates My in the morning always

______________________________.

3 contests never I in take part

______________________________.

4 conductor the Our sometimes chairs tidies

______________________________.

5 Choose the phrases from the box and write 4 more rules for the swimming pool. There are more phrases than you need.

be very quiet | bring a towel with you | clean the floor | eat in the water | run and push people | take a shower before going in | ~~wear a swimming cap~~

SWIMMING POOL RULES

1 You should always wear a swimming cap.
2 ______________________________.
3 ______________________________.
4 ______________________________.
5 ______________________________.

6 Read and write rules for these places. Use should and always or never.

1 Library: You should always be quiet in the library.
2 Museum: ______________________________
3 Park: ______________________________
4 School: ______________________________
5 Your bedroom: ______________________________

7 Think of a place. Say two rules with should always and should never. Can your partner guess the place?

You should never play with a ball here.
You should always listen to your teacher.

Our classroom!

Language lab 2

SHARING OUT TASKS

1 Read. What is Billy going to bring? Check ☑.

crayons ☐ a glue stick ☐ a ruler ☐ cookies ☐

Joe: Billy, can you help me, please? I'm making a poster for my school Drama Club.

Billy: Cool! Should I get some crayons?

Joe: No, thanks. I'm going to use markers and paint.

Billy: OK. Should I bring the glue stick? Maybe you can stick some photos.

Joe: Hmm … No, that's OK. I'm going to draw pictures.

Billy: Well, and a ruler? Do you want me to bring a ruler? You need to write on straight lines.

Joe: I have a ruler here, thanks.

Billy: So, what should I do?

Joe: Can you get me some cookies? I'm hungry!

Billy: OK. Should I help you eat them, too?

Joe: Haha! Yes, good idea!

Should I get some crayons?

Should I bring the glue stick?

Do you want me to bring a ruler?

2 Put more of Billy's questions in order.

1 look for Should I paper some

____________________?

2 photos I these cut Should

____________________?

3 pencil Should a I sharpener bring

____________________?

4 too want me you to bring Do some milk

____________________?

3 Read and write a suggestion with should. Then practice the dialogs with a partner.

1 **A:** It's hot in here.
B: ____________________?

2 **A:** I'm really thirsty.
B: ____________________?

3 **A:** I can't do my homework.
B: ____________________?

4 **A:** My ice-skating equipment is dirty.
B: ____________________?

7 Marvelous medicines

1 Watch. How many sentences do the players get right in time? Check ☑.

one sentence	☐	three sentences	☐
two sentences	☐	zero sentences	☐

2 Read and match. Then complete with the correct form of the word. Watch to check.

check see stop

1 A doctor uses a thermometer
2 Dentists use X-rays
3 Doctors use pills

a ______________ headaches.
b ______________ your temperature.
c ______________ inside your teeth.

3 What's the best treatment for each problem? Check ☑. Say in pairs.

CODE CRACKER

	take a pill	use some cream	use a thermometer	use a bandage	get an X-ray
stomachache	☐	☐	☐	☐	☐
sore throat	☐	☐	☐	☐	☐
temperature	☐	☐	☐	☐	☐
sore shoulder	☐	☐	☐	☐	☐

When you have a stomachache, take a pill.

Language lab 1

TO DO SOMETHING

I will learn to explain why we do something.

1 Read. Write the names next to the photos.

__________ is a dentist.

__________ is a doctor.

I'm Louisa and I see many patients every day. First, I use soap to clean my hands from germs and then I check the patient. I use a tool called a stethoscope to listen to my patient's heart. If the patient has a cough, I also use it to listen to his or her breathing. I ask the patient questions like "Where does it hurt?" and "When did it start hurting?" I use my computer to write about my patient's problems and then I choose the right medicine for my patients.

My name's Eva and I see many children every day. I have a special light to look into their mouths. I always wash my hands, but I also wear gloves to touch their face and mouth because there are germs. I don't often give my patients medicine. Only if a tooth is very sore. I always tell children that they should take care of their teeth. I use a toothbrush and toothpaste to show them how they should brush their teeth.

2 Read again. Why do they use these tools? Match the photos to the reasons.

1  ☐

2  ☐

3 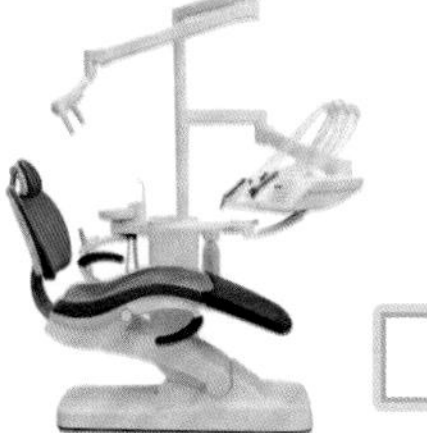 ☐

4 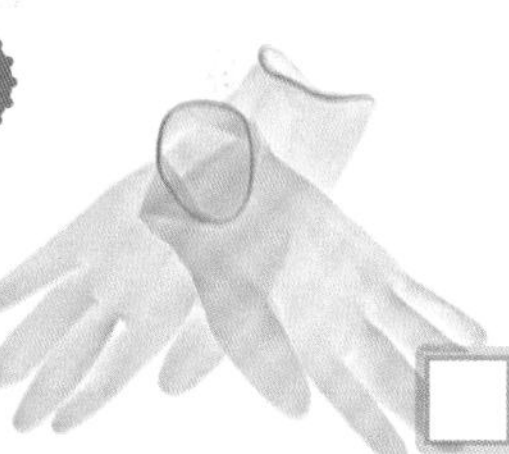 ☐

a to clean her hands

b to touch her patient's face and mouth

c to listen to her patient's heart

d to look into her patient's mouth

Doctors use pills **to stop** headaches.

Why do dentists use water?
To clean your mouth.

3 Read again. Underline the action words with to that explain something.

4 Match the questions and answers.

1 Why do doctors use a bandage?
2 Why are you wearing a hat?
3 Why did you take a pill?
4 Why do you need a thermometer?
5 Why do dentists use X-rays?

a To check my temperature.
b To keep my head warm.
c To see your teeth.
d To cover a cut.
e To stop my headache.

5 Complete with to and the phrases in the box.

make us soup make your throat better put on my sore skin stop his cough wash our clothes

1 We use a special soap ______________________.
2 Fred took some medicine ______________________.
3 Can you buy some cream ______________________, please?
4 Would you like some tea ______________________?
5 Dad needs some carrots and a lemon ______________________.

6 Make sentences about each photo. Then share with a partner and guess.

1 
2 
3 
4 

______________________ ______________________ ______________________ ______________________
______________________ ______________________ ______________________ ______________________

I use them to keep my feet warm.

Socks!

7 Design a gadget that you can use for different things. Draw it on paper and say what you can use it for.

This is my gadget. It's called "Multipencil." You can use it to write and to draw pictures. You can use it to cut paper and to measure things.

Language lab 2

MY HEAD HURTS!

I will ask and answer about illnesses.

1 Read. What is Harry's problem? Check ☑.

a sore throat ☐ a sore knee ☐
a temperature ☐ a headache ☐

Dad: Come on, Harry! Time to get up. You need to get the bus to go to school.
Harry: I can't, Dad.
Dad: Why? What's the matter?
Harry: I have a headache. I don't want to go to school.
Dad: Let's see. Well, you don't have a temperature. Does your throat hurt? Or your ears?
Harry: No, no, they don't.
Dad: OK. Should I call Dr. Smith? Maybe she'll give you a pill.
Harry: No, that's OK ... Dad?
Dad: Yes.
Harry: I don't have a headache. Today's the big soccer match, but I can't play. My knee hurts.
Dad: I see. Come on. Let's go and talk to your coach. I can drive you to school.
Harry: Thanks, Dad!

2 Read and circle T (True) or F (False).

1 Harry is in bed. T / F
2 Harry's dad has a headache. T / F
3 Harry has a temperature. T / F
4 Harry's ears don't hurt. T / F
5 Harry is worried about a soccer match. T / F
6 Harry's knee hurts, so he can't play soccer. T / F

My knee **hurts**.
I **have** a headache.
Her throat **doesn't hurt**.
He **doesn't have** a temperature.
Does your knee **hurt**?
Do you **have** a stomachache?

3 Complete with the correct form of have or hurt.

1 My tooth ________________. I need to see my dentist.
2 Silvia ________________ a temperature. She's at school today.
3 **A:** ________________ your eyes ________________ ?
B: No, they don't.
4 **A:** ________________ Hugo ________________ a sore shoulder?
B: Yes, he does.

British
have got

American
have

8 Theme parks

1 Watch. Which words don't you hear? Cross ☒.

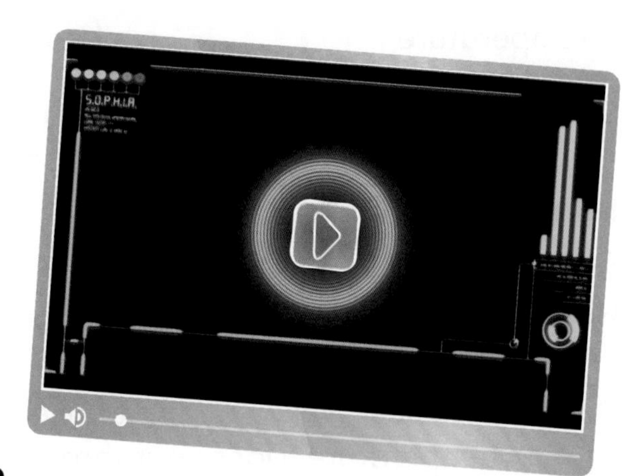

Ferris wheel	☐	theme park	☐
hot dogs	☐	bumper cars	☐
cotton candy	☐	spiral slide	☐
roller coaster	☐	potato chips	☐

2 Read and circle the correct form of the action word. Watch to check.

1 It's 4:00 p.m. Sarah 's going / went / 'll go on the roller coaster at 3:00 p.m.

2 Right now she 's standing / stood / 'll stand in line for cotton candy.

3 At lunchtime, Brian 's waiting / waited / 'll wait for potato chips with his friends.

4 Now he 's leaving / left / 'll leave the park with his friend Tom.

5 He 'going / went / 'll go on the Ferris wheel next time.

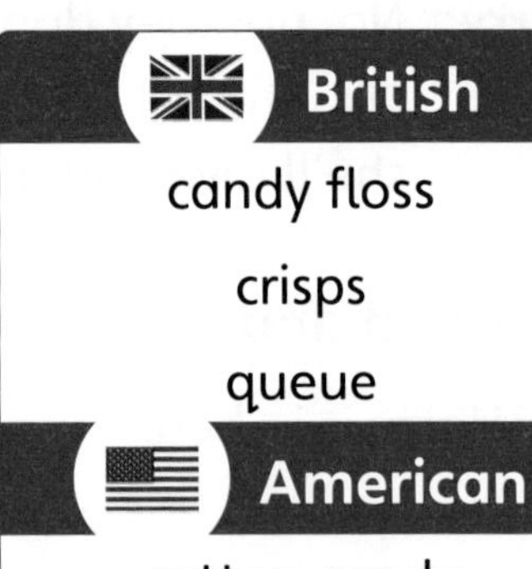

British	American
candy floss	cotton candy
crisps	potato chips
queue	stand in line

3 Look, read, and complete.

CODE CRACKER

1 is eating – ate – is playing – played – is going – ________________

2 drank – will drink – ate – will eat – waited – ________________

3 came – came – will come – watched – watched – ________________

4 will go – is going – went – will ride – is riding – ________________

Language lab 1

PAST, PRESENT, AND FUTURE

I will learn to compare the past, present, and future.

1 Read the interview. What didn't Amy enjoy about her week? Check ☑.

1 She studied a lot. ☐ 2 She practiced the piano. ☐ 3 She didn't paint. ☐

Hi, Amy. How are you?
I'm fine, thanks! It's Friday today, yay!

Did you enjoy your week?
Well, yes, but not all of it. I had a lot of homework on Tuesday and a math test on Wednesday. I also practiced the piano every day after school, but that was fun.

Which day was the best this week?
I enjoyed Thursday because we had art class. We painted a tree. Next week, I'll paint a whale!

What are you doing now?
I'm watching TV with my family and I'm eating a hot dog for dinner.

What about this weekend?
I want to go to the theme park on Saturday. I'll go on the Ferris wheel, but not on the roller coaster.
It's too fast and I'm scared!

2 Read again. Circle T (True) or F (False).

1 Amy likes Fridays. T / F
2 She had a test in English on Wednesday. T / F
3 She's eating breakfast now. T / F
4 She won't go on a roller coaster on Saturday. T / F

When **did** you **go** there?	What **is** she **doing** now?	What **will** they **buy**?
We **went** there yesterday.	She**'s watching** TV.	They **will buy** hot dogs.
You **didn't go out** today.	**I'm not reading** now.	We **won't eat** popcorn.
Did he **like** the movie? Yes, he **did**. / No, he **didn't**.	**Is** Katie **sleeping**? Yes, she **is**. / No, she **isn't**.	**Will** you **go** to the **park?** Yes, I **will**. / No, I **won't**.

3 Read again. Underline the action words in the past in green, in the present in blue, in the future in red.

4 Match the questions to the answers.

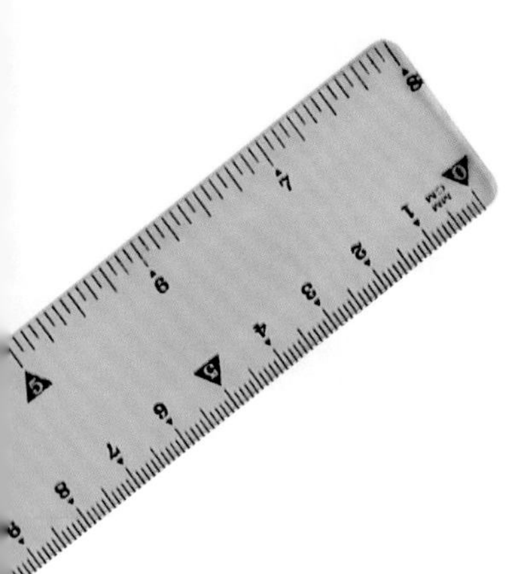

1 What are you doing now?
2 What will you do this weekend?
3 What did you do last weekend?

a I'll go to the theme park with my friends.
b I went to the museum with my parents.
c I'm doing my English homework.

5 Complete the sentences with the correct forms of the action words.

go listen scream stand work

1 My grandpa ________________ at a theme park when he was young.
2 **A:** Why ________________ they ________________ ?
B: Because they are scared.
3 Sorry, I can't hear you because I ________________ to music.
4 Alex and Sarah ________________ in line for a long time because a lot of people want to go on the bumper cars, too.
5 **A:** ________________ you ________________ on the roller coaster last weekend?
B: No, we didn't. The lines were too long.

6 Write three questions to ask your partner. Take turns asking and answering.

Present (*be* + action word *-ing*)

1 ____ ?

Past

2 ____ ?

Future *will*

3 ____ ?

What are you reading at the moment?

I'm reading a book about the best theme parks in the world. My friend gave it to me.

Language lab 2

EXPRESSING FEELINGS

I will express my feelings.

1 Read. Check ☑ the best suggestion for Matthew.

Hi everybody! I'm at the airport with my parents. Our plane to Egypt will leave soon. I'm really excited about this vacation because I love Egypt! I'm really interested in pyramids, but I'm scared of planes. I'm worried about flying today because we need to be on a plane for seven hours to get to Egypt ... What can I do?

Matthew, 12

1. Don't go by plane to Egypt. How about traveling by bus and ship? It'll take weeks, but it'll be fun! ☐
2. How about watching a movie or listening to music on the plane? It'll help you relax and forget about where you are. ☐
3. You can stay at home or go somewhere closer. What about a lake near your town? You don't need to travel to other countries. ☐

2 Read again. Match.

1	Matthew's excited	a	of planes.
2	He's really interested	b	about his vacation in Egypt.
3	He's scared	c	about flying.
4	He's worried	d	in Egyptian pyramids.

3 Complete the sentences for you. Compare with a partner and give suggestions using How about ...ing? or What about ...?

1 I'm scared of ______________________.
2 I'm worried about ______________________.
3 I'm interested in ______________________, but ______________________.
4 I'm excited about ______________________, but ______________________.

I'm scared of the roller coaster.

We can go on a different ride. What about the Ferris wheel?

I'm **excited about** the trip.
She's **interested in** science.
We are **scared of** flying.
They are **worried about** exams.
How about watch**ing** a movie?
What about some popcorn?

Extra Grammar 1

MYSELF / YOURSELF / HERSELF / OURSELVES / THEMSELVES

I will use reflexive pronouns to talk about events.

1 Read the dialog. Check ☑ the equipment that Jack used.

compass ☐ knife ☐ map ☐ rope ☐ whistle ☐

Anna: Hi, Jack! I didn't see you on Sunday. Where were you?

Jack: Hi, Anna! I was orienteering.

Anna: Orienteering? What's that?

Jack: Well, it's a kind of race. You need to run in the forest using a compass and a map. And you need to go from one place to another. The first person to finish is the winner.

Anna: It sounds easy.

Jack: Well, it isn't! I needed to teach myself to use a compass and to read a map first. I also trained myself to walk five kilometers in an hour. An easy race takes about two hours.

Anna: Do you need any special equipment?

Jack: You need good walking shoes, a hat, and a bottle of water. The only special equipment is a compass, a map, and a whistle.

Anna: What's the whistle for?

Jack: You need a whistle if you get lost or hurt yourself. My brother, Eric, hurt himself at a race last month. He could call for help with his whistle.

2 Read again. Write T (True) or F (False).

1 In orienteering, you need to be fast. ____
2 You need to use a compass, but you can't use a map. ____
3 Jack taught himself how to read a map before the race. ____
4 Jack can walk five kilometers in an hour. ____
5 Jack helped his brother when he got hurt. ____

I	→	**myself**
you	→	**yourself**
he	→	**himself**
she	→	**herself**
it	→	**itself**
we	→	**ourselves**
you	→	**yourselves**
they	→	**themselves**

3 Read again. Underline myself/yourself/... and the action words that go with them.

4 Circle the correct word.

1 Alex is four years old and he can dress myself / himself now.
2 Did you enjoy yourself / you at the party?
3 I cut me / myself when I was making a sandwich.
4 We had to dry yourself / ourselves after walking in the rain.
5 My cat taught itself / myself to open the door.
6 Alex and Sara were hungry, so they made yourselves / themselves a sandwich.

5 Complete the sentences with the correct word.

1 I never cook __________ breakfast in the mornings.
2 Ben always enjoys __________ at parties.
3 Mary, be careful! You'll cut __________ !
4 My brother and I want to build __________ a treehouse.
5 Please help your sister wash __________ . Her face and hands are dirty.
6 You and Natalie are old enough to make __________ a sandwich.

6 Complete the sentences with your own ideas. Then compare in groups.

1 I want to teach myself how to ______________________________ .
2 My friend hurt himself/herself when ______________________________ .
3 Children should always wash themselves before ______________________________ .
4 My classmates enjoy themselves when ______________________________ .
5 I started to dress myself when I was ______________________________ .

I want to teach myself how to skate.

Cool. I want to teach myself how to make a cake.

Extra Grammar 2

WOULD AND WOULD LIKE

I will make polite requests and offers using ***would*** *and* ***would like.***

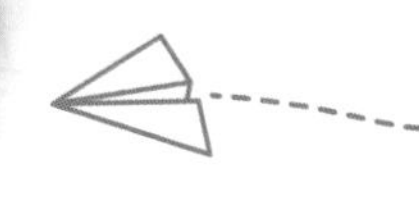

1 **Read the birthday rhyme. How many party words can you find? Underline them.**

JULIA'S BIRTHDAY PARTY

For my birthday, I want a big party.
Would you like balloons?
Yes, please. Balloons are pretty.

For my birthday, I want a big party with balloons.
I want to sing songs and dance with my friends.
Would you dance with us, Dad?
Sorry, I can't. I don't dance very well.

Would you like to play party games, too?
Yes, I would! Party games are very, very good!
For my birthday, would you make me good food?
OK! How about some hot dogs and potato chips?
Yes, please! Please make me a cake, too!

You can't have a party without friends.
At my party, I need my friends from the start to the end!

2 **Read and circle would you or would you like.**

1 Would you / Would you like a birthday party?
2 Would you / Would you like buy some balloons?
3 Would you / Would you like sing a birthday song?
4 Would you / Would you like potato chips or cake?
5 Would you / Would you like to dance with me?

Requests	**Offers**
Would you buy balloons for my party?	**Would** you **like** a hot dog?
Would you make a big cake?	Yes, **I would**. / Yes, **please**.
Yes, sure! / **Sorry**, I can't.	No, **thanks**. / No, **thank you**.

3 **Read again. Underline the requests in green and the offers in blue.**

4 Complete with would or would like and the words in parentheses.

1 ___________ you ____________________ (a sandwich)? I can make you one.
2 ___________ you ____________________ (come) to my party, please?
3 ___________ you ____________________ (some water)? You look thirsty.
4 ___________ you ____________________ (to eat) something? There's chicken or fish.
5 ___________ you ____________________ (bring) me some cake? I want to try it.
6 ___________ you ____________________ (play) with me after school, please?

5 Order the requests and offers. Then circle R (request) or O (offer).

1 Would me you give please juice some
____? R / O

2 to the Would us drive party you
____? R / O

3 like you lunch Would pasta for
____? R / O

4 Would the you salad make
____? R / O

5 hat like Would new a you
____? R / O

6 you pasta like on your Would cheese
____? R / O

6 Think of three requests and write them down. Tell your partner.

1 Would you ____________________________________?
2 Would you ____________________________________?
3 Would you ____________________________________?

Would you open the window, please?

Yes, sure.

7 Think of three offers and write them down. Tell your partner.

1 Would you like some ____________________________?
2 Would you like to ______________________________?
3 Would you like some ____________________________?

Would you like to go to the park with me?

Great idea! Let's go.

Extra Grammar 3

MORE SLOWLY AND *THE MOST SLOWLY*

I will use language to compare animals.

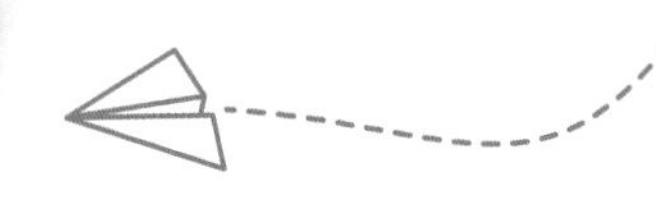

1 Read. Which animal is the fastest? Check ☑.

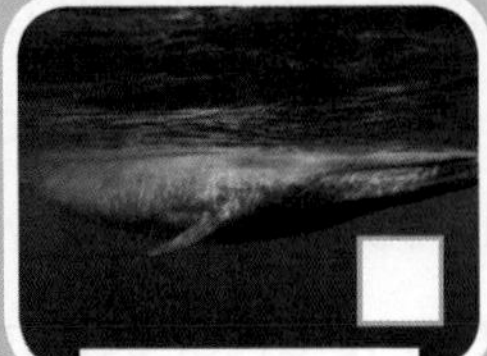

blue whale

cheetah

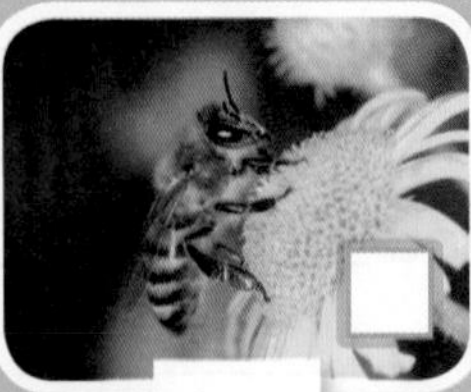

bee

sloth

There are a lot of animals that can move more quickly than humans. The animal that can run the fastest is the cheetah. It runs at 120 kilometers per hour – more quickly than any other land animal.

In the sky, the bird that flies the fastest is the peregrine falcon. It can fly down at about 320 kilometers per hour! That's fast!

The animal that moves the most slowly on land is the sloth, it can only travel at about 2 meters a minute!

The animal that can make the most noise is the blue whale – it sings more loudly than an airplane.

Some people think fish are the animals that move the most quietly. They don't make much noise at all when they swim.

The animal that works the hardest is probably the bee. It never stops moving or looking for food. Maybe that's why we say someone is "as busy as a bee" when he or she works a lot.

2 Read again and match.

1 Bees
2 Cheetahs
3 Sloths
4 Blue whales
5 Fish

a move more quietly than other animals.
b work harder than any other animal.
c run faster than other animals.
d call more loudly than any other animal.
e move more slowly than other animals.

3 Read again. Underline words describing actions with more/-er and circle words describing actions with the most/-est.

fast	faster	**the** fast**est**
slow**ly**	**more** slow**ly**	**the most** slow**ly**

4 Read and choose.

1 Sloths move more slowly / the most slowly than other animals.
2 The peregrine falcon flies faster / the fastest than a cheetah runs.
3 Bees work harder / the hardest than butterflies.
4 The cheetah can run faster / the fastest of all land animals.
5 Blue whales sing more loudly / the most loudly of all animals.

5 Complete the sentences using words describing actions with more/-er or with the most/-est.

1 A hamster can run ______________________ (fast) than a sloth.
2 A cheetah moves ______________________ (slowly) than a peregrine falcon.
3 Fish move ______________________ (quietly) of all animals.
4 A frog can jump ______________________ (high) than a snail.
5 Bees work ______________________ (hard) than any of the other animals.
6 Falcons fly ______________________ (quickly) of all birds that we know.

6 Play a guessing game in groups. Choose an animal and describe what it can do. Use some words describing actions. Can your partners guess the animal?

fast hard high quickly slowly

It moves on the ground. It moves more quickly than a snail. It's dangerous.

Is it a snake?

Yes, it is!

Grammar Reference

Unit 1

Language lab 1

Going to for immediate future (affirmative and negative statements and question form):

She *is going to* buy a book. She *isn't going to* buy a blanket.
He *is going to* go to the market. He *isn't going to* go to the bakery.
They *are going to* buy apples. They *aren't going to* buy mangoes.

Are you *going to* buy some cakes?
No, I'm not.

Are you *going to* meet your friends?
Yes, I am.

Language lab 2

Prepositions of time:

What time are you meeting your friends?
At 11 o'clock.

How long are you going to stay at the mall?
For three hours.

When are you going to go to the supermarket?
On Thursday.

When are you going to go to the mall again?
In a few weeks.

Unit 2

Language lab 1

Comparing the Simple Past and Simple Present (affirmative and negative statements):

She *rides* her bike, she *doesn't take* the bus. She *wears* warm clothes.
They all *play* soccer after school.
They *don't play* basketball.

She *rode* her bike, she *didn't take* the bus. She *wore* warm clothes.
They all *played* soccer after school.
They *didn't play* basketball.

Language lab 2

Using _could_ and _ago_ to talk about abilities in the past:

When *could* you play soccer?
I *could* play soccer when I was six.
That's four years *ago*.

When *could* you ride a bike?
I *couldn't* ride a bike two years *ago*.
I learned to ride a bike last year.

Unit 3

Language lab 1

Will **for predictions (affirmative and negative statements and question form):**

Will we go to school in the future?
No, we *won't* go to school. We *will* study at home. We *won't* sit in a classroom. We *will* study in our bedroom.

Will we have a teacher?
Yes, we *will*.

Will we play sports?
No, we *won't*.

Language lab 2

Will **with** ***wh-*** **questions:**

When will we study?
We *will* study in the evenings.

How will we communicate with our teacher?
We *will* talk to our teacher on a computer screen.

What will we study?
We *will* study recycling and learn to grow food.

Who will we talk to?
We *will* talk to our friends on weekends.

Where will we meet our friends?
We *will* meet them in the park.

Unit 4

Language lab 1

Past Progressive (affirmative and negative statements and question form):

Yesterday, I *was making* a camp with my friends.
We *were exploring* the forest.
Ali *was cooking*. He *wasn't collecting* leaves.
Maya and Leon *were climbing* trees. They *weren't doing* their homework.
Was Ali *using* a knife?
No, he *wasn't*.
Was he *cooking* rice?
Yes, he *was*.
Were Maya and Leon *wearing* gloves?
Yes, they *were*.
Were they *using* a rope?
No, they *weren't*.

Language lab 2

Simple Past with the Past Progressive:

What *were* you *doing* when it *started* to rain?
I *was swinging* from a tree when it *started* to rain. I *wasn't wearing* a coat!
My friends *were eating* when it *started* to rain.
They *weren't cooking*.

Grammar Reference

Unit 5

Language lab 1

First Conditional:

If they *compost* the kitchen waste, it *will rot*.
If they *reuse* glass jars and plastic bottles, there *will be* less waste.
If they *walk or cycle*, there *won't be* as much pollution.
If they *don't recycle*, they *won't protect* the environment.

Language lab 2

More than / Fewer than:

There are *fewer* glass bottles *than* plastic bottles.
There are *more* metal cans *than* paper to recycle.
Are there *more* glass jars *than* shopping bags? Yes, there are.
Are there *fewer* flowers *than* trees? No, there aren't. There are *more*.

Unit 6

Language lab 1

***Should* for obligations:**

You *should* do your homework.
You *shouldn't* be late for school.
You *should* listen to the teacher.
You *shouldn't* talk in class.

Adverbs of frequency (*always, often, sometimes, never*):

I *always* do my homework.
We *often* practice playing music.
She *sometimes* tidies her bedroom.
He *never* takes out the trash.

Language lab 2

Making suggestions with *Should I ...? / Do you want me to ...?* :

Should I make lunch?
Yes!

Do you want me to get everyone a drink?
Good idea! It's been a really hot day.

Unit 7

Language lab 1

Infinitives of purpose:

We eat ice cream *to keep* us cool.
We wear sunglasses *to protect* our eyes.
We use cream *to stop* the sun burning our skin.

Language lab 2

Talking about illnesses:

My head *hurts*. I have a *headache*.
My back *doesn't hurt*. I don't have a *backache*.
His ear *hurts*. He has an *earache*.

Does your stomach *hurt*?
Yes, it does.

Do you have a *stomachache*?
Yes, I do.

Unit 8

Language lab 1

Talking about the past, present, and future using the Simple Past, Present Progressive, and Future with *will*:

This morning, she *learned* about endangered animals.
She *saw* some rare turtles.
She *is having* a picnic.
She *is drinking* juice and *eating* a sandwich.
After lunch, she *will see* the elephants.
She *won't see* any eagles.

Language lab 2

Expressing feelings (*scared of …, interested in …, worried about …, excited about …*):

How about going to see the wolves?
Oh no! I'm *scared of* wolves.
What about the giraffes?
OK. I'm *interested in* giraffes.
I'm *worried about* the tigers because they are endangered.
I'm *excited about* the bears.
They're my favorite animals!

Pearson Education Limited
KAO TWO
KAO Park
Hockham Way
Harlow, Essex
CM17 9SR
England

and Associated Companies throughout the world.

english.com/englishcode

First published 2021
Second impression 2022

ISBN: 978-1-292-35454-5

Set in Heinemann Roman 12pt
Printed in Slovakia by Neografia

Image Credits:

123RF.com: Cathy Yeulet 23, 31, 35, Dmitri Stalnuhhin 32, elenathewise 31, Eric Isselee 43, Ignasi Such 42, Mikalai Manyshau 16, Paul Wolf 25, Peter Jurik 15, Samuel Micut 28, Sergeydv 16, Stockyimages 11, Suljo 31, Sunabesyou 27, Рыбалтовская Марина 43; **Getty Images:** Mima Foto/ EyeEm 10, 17, 23; **Pearson Education Ltd:** Jon Barlow 3, 6, 16, 24, 32, 36, 39; **Shutterstock.com:** 1443815 43, 386866 9, Andrew Sutton 42, Anuradha Marwah 22, Arnoud Quanjer 42, Beth Swanson 22, Brent Hofacke 39, Chris Hill 42, Creatista 8, DM7 16, Dmitry Naumov 7, Eric Isselee 43, GaudiLab 11, Holly Kuchera 22, IM_photo 13, Jojje 32, Keren 7, Kiwis 13, Lopolo 4, 40, Lukas Gojda 5, 6, 10, 17, 18, 23, 33, 37, Maciej Olszewski 42, Mega Pixel. 7, 18, Mikhail Tchkheidze 29, Nataliia Melnychuk 7, oksana2010 31, Ollyy 11, Photomaster 43, Ramon Espelt Photography 10, 23, Richard Peterson 43, Sabphoto 33, Sari ONeal 22, Sashkin 31, sassystock 19, Sergey Novikov 36, SergeyDV 17, Sergiy Zavgorodny 38, Serhii Bobyk 7, Solis Images 31, Stockphoto Mania 43, Syda Productions 13, Tale 32, timquo 15, 17, 31, 39, Tyler Olson 21, Valkoinen 32, Yevgeniy11 43

Video Screenshots: Jungle Creative

Cover Images: Front: **Pearson Education Ltd:** Jon Barlow; Shutterstock. com: Rawpixel.com